# THE 12 LAWS

# OF WEALTH BUILDING

## A Proven Step-by-Step System for Building Wealth and Achieving Financial Independence

## Robert Malone

*Financial Advisor • CPA • Wealth Builder*

# Copyright

# Table of Contents

# Dedication

To my father,

**Donell Malone**

Born in 1926 to sharecropper parents in Alabama, he began picking cotton at five years old.

Hard work was not a choice for him, it was survival.

He did not grow up with opportunity. He created it.

He did not leave me an inheritance of money. He left me something far more valuable— a command:

"Get this family out of poverty."

Those words were not spoken casually.

They were spoken with fire, conviction, and hope. They became my mission.

Every discipline I developed, every risk I took,

every long night studying, every business built, every investment made—was rooted in that charge.

My father passed away when I was thirty years old, just as I became a millionaire.

He never saw what I became.

But everything I became was because of him.

Dad, this book is a testament to your belief, your sacrifice,

and your vision for something greater than yourself.

**You started it all.**

# Preface

## Why Do So Few Americans Become Wealthy?

Why do so few Americans become wealthy?

This question matters—because on the surface, it makes no sense. Americans live in the richest country in the world.

They earn some of the highest incomes on earth.

They have access to opportunity, education, and capital unmatched in history. And yet, only about **4% of Americans ever achieve true financial independence.** The rest spend their lives working, worrying, and hoping things improve.

But things rarely do.

I began studying wealth creation in 1980. At that time, approximately 4% of Americans achieved financial independence.

Fifty years later, that number has not meaningfully changed.

## The Financial Reality Most People Avoid

Most Americans are in a financially vulnerable position. Consider the reality:

- Over 60% live paycheck to paycheck, including high earners
- Nearly half cannot handle a $500 emergency without borrowing
- Millions have no retirement savings
- Average savings fall far short of financial independence
- Consumer debt steadily erodes future wealth These problems affect the majority—not a small minority.

## Why Hard Work Isn't Enough

This problem does not come from a lack of effort. Most people work hard.

Many work extremely hard.

The real issue is more fundamental—and rarely addressed:

Most people were never taught how wealth is actually created.

They were taught to:

- earn
- spend
- borrow
- hope

They were not taught:

- how money works
- value creation
- compounding habits
- paying themselves first
- rational investing

Effort without direction produces very little.

## A Lifetime Spent Studying Wealth

At age 24, shortly after graduate business school, I began seriously studying how wealth is truly built—not casually or academically, but deliberately.

I studied:

- entrepreneurs
- investors
- business owners
- men who built lasting fortunes—not just income
  Over time, one truth became undeniable:

**Wealth obeys laws.**

## When I Applied the Laws

After learning those laws, I applied them intentionally. I saved aggressively.

I created multiple income streams. I invested rationally.

I made disciplined decisions. I exercised patience.

By age 31, I became a millionaire. Not through speculation.

Not through inheritance.

Not through shortcuts. Through laws.

Since then, I have accumulated significant wealth for myself and my family—and protected it through prudent, long-term decision-making.

## Why This Book Exists

The purpose of this book is simple:

To teach wealth-building laws to those who were never shown them.

By learning and applying these laws, financial independence becomes achievable—not hopeful or accidental.

These principles are grounded in real-world results. When followed consistently, wealth becomes predictable.

## What This Book Will Give You

This book provides:

- clarity instead of confusion
- discipline instead of aimlessness
- principles instead of guesswork

When applied with patience and intentional action, these principles can transform your financial life—just as they transformed mine.

Anyone who understands and follows the rules can build wealth.

# The Wealth Builder's Manifesto

**A Stoic Declaration of Financial Sovereignty**

Wealth is not granted. It is earned.

It is not a gift of luck.

It is not a reward for effort alone.

It is the result of alignment with reality. Reality governs all outcomes.

Income follows value.

Value follows skill.

Skill follows discipline.

Discipline follows choice.

No one is coming to build your wealth for you. The market does not respond to hope.

It responds to production.

The world does not compensate for intention. It compensates for results.

If you violate economic laws, consequences follow. If you obey them, progress follows.

This is not philosophy. It is structured.

**Wealth is built by individuals who:**

- establish a clear objective
- confront reality objectively
- assume complete accountability
- generate measurable value
- acquire essential competencies
- operate with precision
- cultivate disciplined routines
- maintain consistent productivity
- invest prudently
- leverage compounding over time
- protect a supportive environment
- apply sound judgment

There is no shortcut.

Only alignment—or misalignment.

Wealth is built slowly. Decision by decision. Habit by habit.

Year by year.

Impatience destroys compounding. Emotion destroys capital.

Foolishness destroys opportunity. Wisdom preserves all three.

The disciplined individual becomes steady. Steadiness becomes leverage.

Leverage becomes independence.

Financial independence is not loud. It is calm.

Measured. Controlled.

The individual who governs thoughts, habits, and capital governs the future. Nothing external can substitute for this.

The laws are fixed.

Follow them, and wealth becomes predictable. Ignore them, and struggle becomes inevitable.

The choice is yours. Live aligned.

Build deliberately.

Remain disciplined.

Let time do its work.

And when the years pass—as they always do— you will either stand financially free,

or face the quiet cost of having ignored the laws.

# Introduction

## Wealth Is Not an Accident

Most people believe wealth is complicated.

They assume it requires special intelligence, lucky breaks, the right connections, or an unusually high income.

They are wrong.

Wealth is not mysterious. Wealth is governed by law.

Just as gravity governs the physical world, specific principles govern the economic world. You can ignore them. You can misunderstand them. You can violate them.

But you cannot escape them.

If you step off a building, gravity does not negotiate.

If you violate the laws of wealth, poverty does not negotiate either.

I did not grow up wealthy.

I was born into a family rooted in the cotton fields of Alabama. My father, Donell Malone, began picking cotton at five years old. He did not study financial theory. He did not speak in the language of markets, returns, or balance sheets.

But he understood something many educated people never grasp: Reality does not bend for anyone.

If you worked hard but wasted money, you stayed poor. If you earned income but failed to save, you stayed stuck.

If you blamed others for your condition, nothing changed.

He decided early in life that poverty would not be in our permanent condition. And he taught me a principle that shaped everything that followed:

"If you want a different life, you must live by different principles."

Not wishes. No excuses. Principles.

He didn't call them laws.

But that's exactly what they were.

Over the following decades—as a CPA, financial advisor, entrepreneur, and real estate investor—I saw the same pattern repeat.

Some people earned large incomes and built nothing. Others earned modest incomes and quietly became wealthy.

The difference was never luck. It was never background.

It was not raw intelligence. It was alignment.

Alignment with reality. Alignment with responsibility. Alignment with production.

Alignment with discipline.

Those who align with the laws rise.

Those who violate them struggle—regardless of income.

Many high-income earners are broke.

Many average earners become financially independent.

The difference is not income.

The difference is obedience to principles.

Wealth leaves clues. It follows structure.

It responds to discipline.

It compounds through consistent, rational action. It does not respond to hope.

 This book exists for one reason:

To make the laws explicit. Clear.

Structured.

Step-by-step.

So, you stop guessing about wealth building.

These Twelve Laws are not motivational slogans. They are not theories.

They are not trends.

They are observations drawn from decades of watching what works—and watching what fails.

They explain:

- why most people struggle financially
- why income alone does not create wealth
- why debt quietly destroys momentum
- why discipline outperforms intelligence
- why production is the engine of prosperity
- how to systematically build wealth yourself

Not through hype.

Not through shortcuts.

But through law.

You are not behind. You are not incapable.

You were simply never taught the laws. Now you will be.

Wealth is not reserved for the fortunate.

It is built by those who understand and obey the principles that govern it.

The economic world is not chaotic. It is structured.

 It rewards production. It rewards discipline.

It rewards responsibility.

It rewards alignment with reality.

If you choose to live by these laws, your financial life will change. Not because of motivation.

Not because of inspiration.

But because laws work.

You cannot break them.

You can only break yourself against them—or rise by aligning with them.

This book will show you how to rise.

## Why You Can Trust This Framework

I did not stumble into wealth. I built it deliberately.

There was no lottery ticket. No inheritance.

No sudden windfall. There was discipline.

There were quiet decisions no one applauded.

There were nights when others spent freely, and I chose to save.

There were chances to upgrade my lifestyle, and I chose to invest instead.

There were moments when short-term pleasure tempted me—and long-term freedom to win. I remember the day clearly.

I was thirty-one years old.

I wasn't standing on a stage. There was no announcement. No applause.

No headlines.

 Just numbers on a page.

Assets exceeded one million dollars. There was no rush of excitement.

There was certainty.

Certainty that principles work. Certainty that discipline compounds.

Certainty that reality rewards alignment.

That number was not built in a year.

It was built through small, repeated decisions.

Saving became a priority long before it felt comfortable. Investing became routine long before it felt exciting.

Production became non-negotiable.

Financial independence is not created in a single dramatic moment. It is created in thousands of quiet ones.

It comes from choosing long-term strength over short-term gratification—again. Great achievements require patience.

Wealth demands the same.

When the right steps are followed consistently, the outcome becomes predictable.

And since that day, by continuing to apply these same laws, I have grown my wealth substantially— not because I am extraordinary, but because laws do not expire.

They worked then.

They work now.

And they will work for you.

**How to Read This Book**

Do not rush this book.

Each chapter introduces a law that deserves careful thought.

 Read with a pen.

Question your habits.

Be honest about your decisions.

Wealth is not built through inspiration.

It is built by understanding these principles and applying them consistently through rational action over time.

## What Comes Next

In the chapters ahead, you will discover:

- the necessity of defining desire
- how reality directs effort
- the power of personal responsibility
- the role of value and skill in income
- the discipline of saving
- practical investing methods
- the importance of patience, environment, and judgment

This book is written for those who want truth and a structured system for building lasting wealth. These are the principles I used to become wealthy.

They work.

Let's begin.

## Before We Begin

### What Is a Law?

Before we explore the Twelve Laws of Wealth Building, we must answer a simple question:

### What is the law?

A law is not a suggestion.

A law is not a motivational quote. A law is not an opinion.

A law is a description of how reality works. Gravity is a law.

Cause and effect is a law.

Supply and demand is a law.

You do not vote on laws.

You do not negotiate with them.

You either align with them—or suffer the consequences of ignoring them. If you step off a building, gravity does not ask about your intentions.

It responds to reality.

Wealth operates the same way.

There are principles that govern income, saving, investing, asset ownership, debt, production, and long-term financial growth. These principles operate whether you understand them or not.

You can ignore them.

You can misunderstand them. You can violate them.

But you cannot escape them.

If you consistently spend more than you earn, the law of mathematics will compound against you. If you fail to produce value, the market will not reward you.

If you accumulate debt faster than assets, your financial life will deteriorate.

These outcomes are not bad luck.

They are consequences.

 And consequences follow laws.

The purpose of this book is not to inspire you temporarily. It is to show you how wealth works.

Each law in this book describes a cause-and-effect relationship. When followed, the result is predictable.

When ignored, the result is equally predictable.

Wealth is not random. It is structured.

And once you understand the structure, you gain power. Not power over other people.

Power over your financial life.

The Twelve Laws that follow are not theories.

They are distilled observations from decades of business ownership, financial advising, investing, and watching people either rise—or struggle—based on their alignment with reality.

You are about to learn how wealth truly works.

And once you see it clearly, you will never approach money the same way again.

# Law 1

## The Law of Burning Desire

*"Where there is no vision, the people perish..."*

*— Proverbs 29:18*

**N**apoleon Hill, author of **Think and Grow Rich,** wrote that all achievement begins with desire. He was correct.

Desire is essential to building wealth because it is the starting point of all purposeful action. Without desire, there is no direction.

Without direction, effort scatters.

Desire is the first step toward achieving any meaningful financial goal.

## What Is Desire

In **Think and Grow Rich,** Napoleon Hill defines desire as a strong, burning, and intense craving for a specific goal or objective.

Desire goes far beyond wishing or hoping.

It is a passionate commitment that occupies your thoughts, shapes your decisions, and directs your actions.

It becomes something you organize your life around.

## What Desire Is (According to Hill)

True desire has distinct characteristics:

- **Clear** — You know exactly what you want.
- **Emotional** — Strong feelings are attached to the outcome.
- **Motivating** — It sparks planning and sustained action.
- **Persistent** — It survives difficulty and delay.
- **Identity-level** — You begin to expect the outcome, not merely want it.

Desire is not casual interest.

It is a serious commitment to achieving a specific result.

## Hill's Core Insight

Failure is rarely caused by a lack of intelligence or opportunity.

More often, it comes from a desire that is too weak to organize a person's thoughts, habits, and

actions around a single objective. As Hill observed:

Small desires produce small outcomes.

Burning desires create strength, focus, and endurance.

## Why Desire Must Burn

Weak desire collapses under comfort and distraction—especially when goals lack personal meaning. Only strong, intentional desire survives:

- delay
- uncertainty

- opposition
- fatigue
- temporary setbacks

Burning desire is not emotional excitement. It is unwavering commitment.

It remains steady regardless of mood, motivation, or circumstance.

## Desire as a Guiding Force

Strong desire directs energy by determining:

- what you accept
- what you reject
- what you allow
- what you deny

Without clear desire, choices feel complicated. With it, decisions become simple.

Desire comes **before** discipline. Discipline without desire eventually fails.

This is why habits collapse when motivation is weak—but thrive when motivation is strong.

## Why Most People Lack Burning Desire

Burning desire requires commitment.

To pursue something seriously, you must be willing to:

- define a clear goal
- eliminate distractions
- abandon excuses
- endure discomfort

Many people prefer vague desires because they preserve flexibility. But flexibility weakens focus.

Only specific goals generate sustained determination. Without clarity, motivation fades and progress stalls.

## My Personal Proof

At age 24, I made a firm decision to build wealth and escape financial poverty. I committed fully to becoming wealthy and followed a clear strategy:

- learning valuable, marketable skills
- creating multiple income streams
- practicing discipline in saving
- investing in real estate and stocks

That burning desire shaped how I thought, how I worked, and how I made decisions. It eliminated hesitation and replaced it with purpose.

## The Test of Burning Desire

Ask yourself this question:

**Does your financial goal shape your daily choices?**

If it does not, the desire is likely too weak. A powerful desire:

- establishes priorities
- justifies sacrifice
- sustains persistence

**Wealth creation begins when a clear, burning desire drives purposeful action toward a defined objective.**

Without desire, nothing begins.

With it, progress becomes inevitable.

# Chapter Summary

### Law 1: The Law of Burning Desire

1. All achievement begins with a clearly defined desire.
2. A wish reflects passivity; desire represents a conscious, decisive commitment.
3. Burning desire extends beyond emotion and requires sustained dedication over time.
4. Effective desire must be specific, intentional, and firmly grounded in purpose.
5. Weak desire collapses under adversity, while strong desire persists through delay, opposition, and challenge.
6. Discipline cannot be sustained without genuine desire to drive it.
7. Wealth building begins when desire shapes thought patterns, priorities, and daily actions.
8. If a goal does not influence decisions, it has not yet reached the level of burning desire.

**In summary:**

The path to wealth begins when a clearly defined desire evolves into an unwavering commitment that governs behavior and action.

# Study & Reflection Questions

## Law 1: The Law of Burning Desire

1. Is my goal of building wealth clearly defined, or is it vague and flexible?
2. What specific financial outcome am I fully committed to achieving?
3. Why do I want this outcome?
4. Is my reason strong enough to endure discomfort, delay, and sacrifice?
5. Which comforts or conveniences am I currently unwilling to give up?
6. Do my daily decisions and actions reflect my stated financial goal?
7. If an outside observer evaluated my life, would they see evidence of burning desire?
8. What specific sacrifices am I willing to begin making right now?

# Law 2

## The Law of Reality

*"Some things are in our control and others not."*

*— Epictetus.*

Understanding this law provides powerful insight—not only into wealth building, but into life itself.

If you want to improve your finances, you must begin with an honest assessment of your current situation.

Most financial failure does not come from missed opportunities. It comes from ignoring reality.

Through decades of experience as a CPA, investor, business owner, and financial advisor, I have seen one truth repeated without exception:

**Reality always asserts itself.**

You may negotiate with yourself.

You may justify mistakes.

You may delay decisions.

Reality does not change.

Eventually, it demands a reckoning—often with compounded consequences.

## What Is Reality?

When we say, "Reality says what is, is," we mean this:

Things are exactly the way they are—whether you like them or not, agree with them or not, or understand them or not.

Reality does not argue.

It does not explain itself.

It is not influenced by emotion. It simply exists.

## In Plain Terms

- Reality looks like this:
- If you earn $60,000 a year, that is your income—regardless of how you feel about it.
- If you spend $70,000 a year, you are operating at a deficit—no matter how optimistic you are.
- Heavy debt restricts cash flow, even if debt feels normal.
- Skills the market does not value will not earn income, regardless of effort.
- Reality is objective—like a scoreboard. Arguing with it changes nothing.

## A Simple Analogy

Reality is like gravity.

You can accept it, reject it, ignore it, or criticize it—but it remains unchanged. Money works the same way.

## Why This Law Matters

People usually run into financial trouble not because of bad intentions, but because of false assumptions.

Common thoughts include:

- "Everything will work out."
- "I'll deal with it later."
- "Things are bound to turn around."

But wealth does not respond to hope.

Until you accept reality as it is, meaningful change is impossible. You cannot fix what you refuse to measure.

## One-Sentence Truth

**Reality shows what is, not what should be. Align your decisions with it.**

As Ayn Rand stated:

"Existence exists. Facts are facts—A is A."

In practical terms:

- Math drives money, not emotion.
- Markets reward value, not need.
- Debt always has consequences.
- Skills earn income based on demand, not effort.
- Numbers do not care about excuses.
- People may lie. Numbers do not.

Hope alone changes nothing.

## Where Most People Break from Reality

This is where financial lives are unraveling.

Many people make decisions as if reality's constraints do not apply to them.

Below are the most common patterns I have observed.

### Income vs. Lifestyle

Reality says:

You can only afford what your income supports. Most people say:

"I'll figure it out."

They upgrade houses, cars, and lifestyles before income supports them—assuming raises, bonuses, or future opportunities will close the gap.

Reality does not operate on assumptions.

When lifestyle runs ahead of income, the result is always the same:

**Debt.**

Debt is borrowed time from the future—time repaid with stress, reduced freedom, and lost opportunity.

## Debt Treated as Normal

Reality says:

Debt is a claim for your future labor. Most people say:

"Everyone has debt."

They finance depreciating assets, carry revolving balances, and normalize obligations that follow them for decades.

Debt does not become harmless because it is common. It becomes dangerous because it is ignored.

## Spending Driven by Emotion, Not Numbers

Reality says:

Spending must align with cash flow.

Most people say:

"I deserve this."

Money does not respond to emotion. It responds to arithmetic.

I have watched people earning excellent incomes remain broken because decisions were driven by feelings rather than facts.

Reality keeps score—even when you do not.

## Investing Without Understanding

Reality says:

Risk cannot be eliminated—only managed. Most people say:

"My friend said this was a good investment."

They confuse speculation with investing, panic when markets move against them, and blame others when losses occur.

Reality sends the bill regardless.

## Avoiding the Numbers

Reality says:

What you do not measure, you cannot control. Many people avoid:

- net worth statements
- cashflow tracking
- total debt calculations
- long-term financial projections

Not because the numbers are complex—but because they are uncomfortable. Avoidance does not erase reality.

It only delays the reckoning.

## The Most Dangerous Habit: Reality Evasion

All these behaviors share one trait:

They ignore reality.

People hope instead of plan. Assume instead of calculating. Postpone instead of deciding.

Avoiding reality makes consequences harsher—not softer.

## My Advantage Was Honesty, Not Genius

I did not build wealth by being smarter than others. I built it by confronting reality early:

- income
- spending
- debt
- skill development
- failures
- successes

I adjusted quickly and changed direction based on facts—even when doing so was uncomfortable. Facing reality early accelerates wealth.

Avoiding it extends hardship.

## Reality Is Not the Enemy

Reality is simply what exists.

When you accept it, clarity follows.

Then you can:

- spend intentionally
- cut excess costs
- stay out of destructive debt
- invest carefully
- build valuable skills
- create real value.

## Why People Struggle to See Reality

Jesus made one of the most profound statements ever recorded:

"He who has eyes to see, let him see."

He was not speaking about physical eyesight. He was describing a deeper truth:

People often look directly at reality—and still refuse to see it.

Truth can be present, undeniable, and life-changing—and still ignored. That is the human condition.

## The Cost of Ignoring Reality

Several years ago, my nephew called me.

"Uncle Rob, how do I get started in real estate?"

He earned $100,000 a year as a computer engineer and had $6,000 saved. Smart. Talented. High income.

I gave him one piece of advice:

"Save your money. When you have $30,000 to $40,000 in cash, you'll be ready." He didn't like the answer.

He later told my son I was "old school" and said there was a newer way—one that didn't require

savings.

That was the first mistake.

## Reality Does Not Bend

He bought a $200,000 house needing $50,000 in repairs. The seller rebated $30,000 at closing.

It felt clever. It felt creative.

It felt like beating the system.

Reality does not care how something feels.

The house could not be rented due to major repairs. But the bank still wanted $1,800 per month.

For 16 months, he paid.

Over $30,000 went straight back to the bank—the exact amount rebated at closing.

The "creative financing" vanished.

He was left with a broken house he could not sell.

## What Reality Required

Reality says:

- repairs require cash
- banks require payments
- bad deals do not improve with optimism
- arithmetic always wins

If he had saved first, everything would have changed. With cash:

- negotiation power increases
- repairs happen immediately
- pressure disappears

- opportunity improves

Cash creates leverage.

Debt creates pressure.

## The Hard Lesson

He did not fail due to lack of intelligence.

He failed because he ignored reality.

Real estate is simple:

1. Build surplus
2. Accumulating cash
3. Buy below value
4. Repair quickly
5. Create cash flow

There is no shortcut around surplus.

When you bring cash, sellers listen.

When you bring debt, banks control you.

Reality rewards discipline—not creativity that violates arithmetic.

That is the Law of Reality.

## The Fundamentals of Wealth Building

Wealth building is not complicated. It rests on basic principles:

- spend less than you earn
- save consistently
- invest rationally
- avoid unnecessary debt
- build valuable skills
- apply discipline over time

There is no mystery here.

It is not reserved for geniuses.

It is not hidden on Wall Street.

And yet millions never do it. Why?

Because they refuse to see reality.

## Fantasy Is More Comfortable Than Truth

Many chase illusions:

- quick money
- lottery wins
- speculative surges
- easy fixes

Wealth requires patience, discipline, and responsibility—qualities that make reality uncomfortable.

## Pride and Comfort Create Blindness

The real obstacle is not knowledge.

It is psychological resistance.

To accept reality, one must admit:

- spending habits are a problem
- personal behavior causes outcomes
- discipline is missing
- no one is coming to rescue them

That honesty destroys excuses—and opens the door to freedom.

## The Fundamental Choice

There are only two paths:

Living in illusion
Or living in reality

Every financial decision reflects one or the other. Ignoring reality delays consequences.

Aligning with it creates progress.

The turning point comes when you stop asking:

**"Why is this happening to me?"**

And start asking:

**"What does reality require me to do now?"**

That question has built every durable fortune I have ever seen.

**The Takeaway**

Success comes from aligning your choices with reality. Accepting reality gives you control.

And control is the first step to building wealth.

# Chapter Summary

**Law 2: The Law of Reality**

1.  Reality is impartial, objective, and unalterable.
2.  Facts remain constant regardless of opinions, hopes, or emotions.
3.  Most financial setbacks result from ignoring reality, not from a lack of opportunity.
4.  A sustainable lifestyle must be supported by income; when it is not, debt fills the gap.
5.  Debt represents a claim on future earnings and reduces financial freedom.
6.  Honestly, objective analysis of financial facts is essential—even when uncomfortable.
7.  Wealth accumulation is straightforward once factual circumstances are recognized and accepted.
8.  Ignoring reality delays necessary adjustments and magnifies eventual consequences.
9.  Progress occurs only when decisions are grounded in verifiable facts rather than assumptions.

**In summary:**

Sustainable wealth is built within real-world limits. Progress comes from aligning actions with reality and making decisions based on facts.

# Study & Reflection Questions

**Law 2: The Law of Reality**

1. In which areas of my financial life am I avoiding hard numbers or clear measurement?
2. Does my current lifestyle accurately align with my actual income?
3. What debt obligations are limiting my future flexibility and freedom?
4. Do I regularly track my net worth and cash flow—or do I avoid them?
5. Which financial decision am I postponing because it feels uncomfortable or inconvenient?
6. Am I currently living in financial illusion—or in financial alignment with reality?
7. If reality requires immediate correction, what is the first change I would need to make?

# Law 3

## The Law of Personal Responsibility

*"If you are pained by any external thing, it is not this thing that disturbs you, but your own judgment about it."*

*— Marcus Aurelius, Meditations.*

The previous chapter addressed reality and truth.

This chapter moves one step further—and speaks plainly:

You are responsible for your progress.

You alone are responsible for your wealth.

### Ask Yourself This Question

I once worked with a client whose finances were in disarray. The stress spilled into his home and strained his marriage.

When discussing his situation, he blamed everyone else— his wife, his job, his children, the economy. Everyone but himself.

I asked him a simple question:

"Do you want your life to feel calm—like a flowing river? Because it can."

He paused, then answered confidently:

"Yes."

I replied just as directly:

"You can live that way only by accepting full responsibility for your life—and by refusing to blame

outside forces for internal disorder." That moment revealed the truth clearly. A calm river does not happen by chance.

## The Calm Life Is Chosen

 Marcus Aurelius and Aristotle both recognized a principle largely ignored today:

A calm ordered life is the result of deliberate choice and disciplined effort.

Marcus Aurelius wrote:

"You have power over your mind—not outside events. Realize this, and you will find strength."

Human responsibility ultimately comes down to two things:

- thoughts
- actions

When you attempt to control everything except the only two things you truly possess, disorder follows.

## Aristotle: The Individual as the Origin

In **Nicomachean Ethics**, Aristotle explains that voluntary actions originate within the individual.

Character is not inherited.

It is formed through repeated choices and deliberate action. In simple terms:

Your life flows from your decisions.

If you are struggling financially, Aristotle would argue that your outcomes reflect your choices—not fate or circumstance.

You control your thoughts. You control your actions.

By changing them, balance returns—and life begins to flow calmly, like a gentle river.

## Blame Disrupts Calm

Blame may provide temporary comfort, but it prevents progress.

 My client remained stuck until he accepted responsibility. When he did, control returned—and calm followed.

Marcus Aurelius stated it clearly:

"If you are distressed by anything external, the pain is not due to the thing itself, but to your judgment about it."

Growth—and wealth—begin when excuses are replaced with responsibility.

## Wealth Responsibility Is Personal

Your wealth is your responsibility—not your:

- financial advisor
- CPA
- employer
- spouse

- government

You may seek guidance. You may receive help.

But ownership always rests with you. This is not harsh.

It is empowering.

Because if no one else is responsible, you hold the power to change your outcome.

## Reality Is Unforgiving—and Fair

Reality does not negotiate.

If you do not learn, growth stops.

If you do not save, wealth cannot form.

If you avoid intelligent investing, money stagnates.

These are not opinions. They are facts.

Blaming advisors, markets, or timing produces nothing. Only accurate thinking and honest action produce results. Responsibility cannot be outsourced.

## When You Accept This Law

When you accept full responsibility for building wealth, everything shifts. You stop reacting.

You stop drifting.
You stop depending.

You become the agent of your own success.

True power comes from owning your inner world—and directing your outward actions accordingly.

## The Law Stated Plainly

Take full responsibility for your thoughts, actions, and finances if you wish to build wealth.

Blame creates disorder. Responsibility creates results.

## The Calm River Revisited

I told my client:

"Taking full responsibility for your life allows it to flow smoothly—like a calm river."

This is not motivational language.

It is practical philosophy.

 Your choices define you.

Your thoughts and actions shape your outcomes. Together, they determine your financial future.

When you accept responsibility, direction appears.

When you own your life, wealth becomes possible.

That is the truth.

**The cavalry is you.**

## Chapter Summary

### Law 3: Personal Responsibility

1. Financial order is the result of deliberate, conscious choices—not chance.
2. You control your thoughts and actions; blaming others creates disorder and stagnation.
3. True financial power and stability come only from accepting full responsibility—this cannot be transferred, even to experts.
4. Advisors may provide guidance, but all decisions and outcomes ultimately belong to you.
5. Wealth is built through repeated, responsible decisions made consistently over time.

**Stated simply:**

Blame produces chaos. Responsibility builds wealth.

# Study & Reflection Questions

## Law 3: Personal Responsibility

1. Where in my financial life am I blaming external circumstances instead of my own decisions?
2. What recurring financial problem can be directly traced back to my choices or habits?
3. Do I review my finances regularly—or do I only react when problems arise?
4. Am I delegating responsibility to others while telling myself I am still "in control"?
5. What specific financial action have I been postponing, and why?
6. If my financial life were entirely my responsibility, which would I change immediately?
7. Am I actively shaping my financial condition, or merely reacting to it as it unfolds?

# Law 4

## The Law of Value

### Why the Market Decides Your Income

*"It is not from the benevolence of the butcher, the brewer, or the baker, that we expect our dinner, but from their regard to their own interest."*

*— Adam Smith, The Wealth of Nations*

This law does two critical things. First, it explains what value is.

Second, it explains how value turns into income.

By now, you have done what most people never do. You decided to change.

You faced reality.

You accepted responsibility.

Now comes the question that determines income:

Why does the world pay some people more than others?

The answer is simple—though often uncomfortable.

**The Market Does Not Care How Hard You Work**
The market is not sentimental. It does not reward:

- effort
- intentions

- stress
- exhaustion

The market ignores how hard a task feels and rewards only the value it receives. Understanding this principle eliminates confusion and false hope.

## What the Law of Value Means

The Law of Value states that your income is determined by how much value you create for others— and how effectively you deliver it.

Value comes from solving relevant problems efficiently while being difficult to replace.

According to the Law of Compensation, your earning potential depends on:

- demand for your work
- your level of skill
- how replaceable you are

These are not abstract ideas.

Your income already reflects them.

## Why This Law Explains Every Income Level

Once you understand this law, income differences stop being mysterious. Income increases when:

- your skills become more sought after
- your capabilities improve
- you become harder to replace

Income remains flat when nothing changes.

The law does not judge effort or intention.

It simply responds to what you offer the market.

## The Reason for the Pay Difference Between a McDonald's Employee and an NFL Quarterback

Consider two extremes.

A worker at McDonald's may earn around $12 an hour.

Why?

Because:

- The required skills are simple
- many people can perform the job
- Replacements are easy to find

Now consider an NFL quarterback earning $50–60 million per year. Why such a massive difference?

Because:

- fewer than 60 people worldwide can perform the job at that level
- demand is exceptionally high
- responsibility is enormous
- replacements are nearly impossible

That quarterback has spent roughly 15 years developing those skills through high school, college, and professional play.

You cannot hire quarterbacks off the street.

Scarcity plus responsibility creates value.

And value determines income.

## Lessons Learned from Observing Successes and Failures

As a CPA, I have seen this principle operate consistently and without exception. Consider two individuals who may:

- work the same hours
- exert similar effort
- experience comparable stress

Yet one advances financially while the other remains stagnant.

The difference is not effort.

It is the value they provide—and how easily they can be replaced.

## How I Created Value as a CPA

When I started my CPA firm in 1985, most firms offered the same services:

- basic bookkeeping
- basic tax preparation

I chose a different approach.

I still prepared tax returns, but my focus was on tax-minimization strategies.

I advised clients on how to legally pay the least amount possible.

Clients valued this—because paying taxes is universally unpopular.

I also provided financial planning services focused on:

- budgeting
- saving
- investing

My goal was not mere compliance.

It was helping clients build wealth.

Within three years, I had over 700 clients.

My firm became a cash-generating business producing substantial income each year.

I did not work harder than everyone else.

I created more value.

## The Mistake Most People Make

Many people attempt to increase income by working longer hours.

That usually leads to more stress and fatigue—and little progress.

The breakthrough occurs when you stop asking:

**"How can I work harder?"**

And start asking:

**"How can I create more value?"**

That single shift changes everything.

## How I Applied the Law of Value

I did not increase my income by outworking others. I increased it by intentionally building skills that:

- were highly sought after
- addressed real needs
- carried significant responsibility
- were difficult to replace

Income followed naturally.

## Applying the Law of Value

Ask yourself:

- What does the market need?
- Which skills increase my value?
- How can I become less replaceable?
- What additional responsibility can I take on?

Value is created deliberately—and once established, it compounds.

## Who Would Suffer If You Disappeared?

This is the most honest question you can ask about your current value:

**Who would suffer if you disappeared?**

If you stopped showing up tomorrow and:

- no decisions stalled
- no production stopped
- no revenue stopped

- no structure broke

Then the market is sending a clear—though uncomfortable—message:

You are easily replaceable.

And if nothing breaks without you, no amount of effort alone will ever make you wealthy.

## Why This Question Reveals Income Truths

The market rewards impact—not mere presence.

If your absence does not change outcomes, your value is limited.

High-value individuals are central to decisions, systems, relationships, or judgment.

When they leave, work slows—or stops.

That is what value looks like.

## Replaceability Determines Compensation

Income rises as replaceability falls.

If your role can be filled quickly, cheaply, and with minimal disruption, compensation will always be capped.

If replacing you is:

- expensive
- slow
- risky

Income rises accordingly.

**Boosting Your Value with One Question**

Ask yourself:

- What would stop working if I left?
- Which decisions depend on my judgment?
- What revenue relies on me?
- Which problems do I solve that others cannot?

Strengthen these areas to increase your value.

**The Takeaway**

This law defines:

- what value is
- how it is created
- why income follows it

The market does not pay for your needs. It does not pay for effort.

**It pays for value.**

# Chapter Summary

**Law 4: The Law of Value**

1. The market determines income—not effort and not intention.
2. Value is created by solving problems people genuinely care about.
3. Income depends on three factors:
   - demand for your work
   - your skill in delivering it
   - how difficult you are to replace
4. Scarcity combined with responsibility increases compensation.
5. Effort without value is invisible to the market.
6. Replaceability places a ceiling on income.
7. If nothing breaks when you leave, your current value is limited.
8. Income grows as impact and usefulness increase.

**Stated simply:**

The market pays for value. Income rises as replaceability falls.

# Study & Reflection Questions

**Law 4: The Law of Value**

1. What specific problems do I solve that people genuinely care about?
2. Is my current income limited by low demand for my work—or by high replaceability?
3. If I disappeared tomorrow, what would stop working or break?
4. What responsibilities could I take on that others avoid or are unwilling to accept?
5. Am I attempting to earn more by working harder—or by becoming more valuable?
6. Which skill, if mastered, would most dramatically reduce my replaceability?
7. What deliberate action can I take this year to meaningfully increase my market value?

# Law 5

## The Law of Skills

### Why Mastery Is the Real Currency of Wealth

*"Seest thou a man diligent in his business? he shall stand before kings..."*

*— Proverbs 22:29*

The Law of Value explains why income increases. The Law of Skills explains how it increases.

Here is the distinction most people miss:

Value does not come from knowing something. It comes from mastering something.

Partial knowledge produces average results.

Mastery produces exceptional outcomes—and exceptional income.

### What the Law of Skills Really Means

The Law of Skills is straightforward:

**High income flows to those who master skills the market demands.**

Not those who dabble.
Not those who talk about skills.
Not those who collect books, courses, or credentials.

The market does not reward:

- familiarity
- enthusiasm
- credentials alone

Premium compensation is paid for:

- competence
- sound judgment
- consistency
- excellence

That is the law.

## Why Mastery Changes Everything

Two people can claim the same skill.

One struggles financially.
The other commands high compensation.


Same field.
Same title.
Very different outcomes. The difference is mastery. Mastery means:

- deep understanding rather than surface knowledge
- judgment rather than rigid rule-following
- reliable performance rather than occasional success

Those who reach mastery become:

- dependable
- highly trusted
- difficult to replace

That is what the market rewards.

## Mastery: Hard Lessons, Profitable Gains

I did not build wealth by knowing a little about many things. I built it by mastering a few skills that mattered.

That required:

- sustained focus
- disciplined study
- practical application
- persistence over time

Mastery is slow to develop—but once achieved, it accelerates progress everywhere else.

## How I Learned to Flip Houses—Properly

I began flipping houses shortly after opening my CPA practice. Houston in the 1980s offered ideal conditions:

- little competition
- abundant undervalued properties
- willing lenders

There was only one problem.

I knew nothing about flipping houses.

One evening, I saw a television advertisement for a two-day seminar on house flipping and decided to attend.

The seminar included two large binders—nearly 1,000 pages of material.

Most people skim material like that.

I did not.

I spent six months studying and mastering it.

But knowledge alone is never enough.

So I partnered with one of my clients, a real estate broker.

I provided the financing.

He found the deals.

That partnership lasted ten years.

Together, we profitably flipped more than 350 houses. I did not merely learn about house flipping.

I mastered the process of:

- buying
- repairing
- selling

The profits allowed me to acquire apartment complexes, and I continue to flip profitable properties today.

That is mastery.

## Why Half-Knowledge Keeps People Stuck

Most people live in the middle.

They know enough to feel informed—but not enough to be valuable.

They:

- read passively
- learn superficially
- start but do not finish

Partial knowledge creates false confidence.

The market quietly ignores it.

## The Skills Worth Mastering

Wealth-building skills share common traits.

They:

- solve real problems
- improve with practice
- require judgment
- compound over time


Examples include:

- financial literacy
- decision-making
- sales and persuasion
- leadership
- investing and capital allocation

These are not skills to sample.

They are skills to commit to mastering.

## How to Apply the Law of Skills

Choose one skill that:

- is valued by the market
- you are willing to master
- will remain relevant over time

Then:

- study with intention
- practice consistently
- apply in real situations
- refine continuously

Do not rush the process.

**Mastery pays for a lifetime.**

## The Takeaway: The Value of Mastery

Information is everywhere.
Knowledge is abundant.

But rarity creates value.

The more uncommon your level of mastery, the greater your worth to the market. If you want to build wealth, stop trying to know a little about everything.

 Choose something that matters.

Choose something useful.

And master it.

# Chapter Summary

**Law 5: The Law of Skills**

1. Income growth depends not on knowing many things, but on mastering a few valuable skills.
2. The market rewards mastery—not familiarity, enthusiasm, or credentials alone.
3. Two people can possess the same skill on paper, yet only the one who masters it commands premium income.
4. Mastery is demonstrated through judgment, consistency, and reliable performance under real conditions.
5. Partial knowledge creates false confidence but produces little market value.
6. Wealth-building skills solve real problems, improve with practice, and compound over time.
7. Mastery requires focused study, deliberate practice, and long-term commitment.
8. Once achieved, mastery accelerates progress and pays dividends for a lifetime.

**Stated simply:**

Wealth flows to those who master skills the market values. Knowledge informs—but mastery earns.

# Study & Reflection Questions

**Law 5: The Law of Skills**

1. What skill am I currently dabbling in rather than committing to mastering?
2. Which single skill, if mastered, would most dramatically increase my income?
3. Am I primarily consuming information—or deliberately building real competence?
4. How much focused, deliberate practice have I committed to over the past year?
5. Which marketable skill will still be valuable ten years from now?
6. Where am I mistaking familiarity for true mastery?
7. What specific action can I take this month to deepen mastery in my chosen skill?

# Law 6

## The Law of Work and Production

### Wealth Stems From Production

*"In all labour there is profit: but the talk of the lips tendeth only to penury."*

*— Proverbs 14:23*

Burning desire fuels the will. Reality provides direction.

Responsibility gives control. Value and skills provide leverage.

But none of these produce wealth without work. And here is the truth most people never learn:

Work is not activity. Work is production.

Real work creates value through the production of a defined product or the delivery of a specific service.

## What the Law of Work Really Means

The Law of Work states:

**Work is the disciplined production of a clearly defined product or service—at a defined quality and in meaningful quantity.**

If nothing is produced, no work has occurred.

It is entirely possible to stay busy all day and still produce nothing of value. Emails, meetings, movement, and noise often fill time.

None of it counts unless something tangible is created.

## Why Defining Your Product Changes Everything

Every form of real work has three components:

1. A clearly defined product
2. A clearly defined quality standard
3. A clearly defined quantity

Work begins only after these three are specified. Without a product, work cannot begin.

Without standards, value cannot be judged. Without quantity, income cannot grow.

Most people do not fail because they are lazy.

They fail because they have never clearly defined what they are supposed to be producing.

## Why Undefined Work Produces Unstable Income

If your income feels unpredictable, frustrating, or capped, there is usually one root cause. It is not lack of effort.

It is not lack of ability.

It is lack of clarity.

When clarity is missing:

- deadlines slip
- clients complain
- managers grow frustrated
- income stagnates

Production is unclear—and confusion replaces structure.

## The Hidden Chaos Behind Most Jobs and Businesses

Most people believe work problems come from:

- bad bosses
- lazy coworkers
- unfair systems

- bad luck

That is surface-level thinking.

 At the root of most workplace problems is this:

Someone is producing without knowing **what** must be produced, **how well** it must be produced, or

**how much** must be produced.

That is not work.

That is confusion disguised as effort.

**The Law of Production**

The Law of Production states:

**High income results from consistently producing a clearly defined product, at a clearly defined quality standard, and in a clearly defined quantity.**

Miss one element and income becomes unstable.

Miss two and frustration dominates.

Miss all three and chaos is guaranteed.

**The Three Pillars of Consistent High Income**

Every high-income individual—employee or entrepreneur—masters all three. There are no exceptions.

## 1.  The Product Must Be Defined

The market asks one basic question:

**What do you produce?**

Most people cannot answer clearly.

They say:

- "I work in finance."
- "I'm in real estate."
- "I do consulting."
- "I help people."

These are not products.
They are job-title fog machines.

A product is a specific outcome another person wants.

When the product is vague:

- expectations clash
- value is misunderstood
- compensation becomes negotiable—downward

At work, unclear products cause:

- scope creep

- endless revisions

- chronic misunderstanding

Clear products create calm, focus, and leverage.

## 2.  The Quality Standard Must Be Defined

Even when a product exists, quality is often undefined. People do not know:

- what "excellent" means

- what is acceptable

- when work is complete

This leads to phrases like:

- "This isn't what I wanted."

- "Can you redo this?"

- "That's not quite right."

Quality ambiguity produces:

- rework

- stress

- resentment

- wasted time

High earners do not guess at quality.

They define it upfront—and meet it consistently.

## 3.  The Quantity Must Be Defined

This is the most overlooked pillar—and the one that destroys income consistency.

Even with clear products and high quality, income collapses when quantity is undefined.

Questions like:

- How often?
- How many?
- How fast?
- At what scale?

Go unanswered.

The result:

- unpredictable output
- uneven results
- income spikes followed by droughts

High income is not produced in bursts.

It is produced through repeatable volume.

Quantity creates momentum. Momentum creates leverage.

## Why Problems Explode When One Pillar Is Missing

The pattern is consistent:

- No product definition → confusion
- No quality standard → conflict
- No quantity target → instability

Workplace drama is rarely emotional. It is structural.

When all three are defined, work becomes:

- calmer
- cleaner
- predictable

And income follows structure.

## Why High Earners Look "Effortless"

From the outside, high earners appear relaxed. That is because they are not deciding as they go. They already know:

- what they produce
- how good it must be
- how much must be delivered

Their energy goes into execution—not confusion.

That is why they scale.

That is why they earn more.

## The Market Only Pays for What It Can Measure

The market does not reward:

- vagueness
- intention
- potential

It rewards:

- defined output
- consistent quality
- reliable quantity

When all three are defined, income stops being emotional.

It becomes mechanical.

Predictable.

Repeatable.

## The Turning Point

The moment you define your product, establish quality standards, and set quantity targets:

You stop being busy.
You start being valuable.

And value—produced consistently—always turns into income.

## The Law in One Sentence

**High income is the natural result of clearly defined production—product, quality, and quantity—executed consistently over time.**

Miss one, and problems multiply.
Master all three, and income becomes a system.

## What My Business Taught Me About Real Work

In my tax preparation business, I learned this early:

I had to define my product.

My product was not "working on taxes."

My product was:

**An accurately prepared tax return, fully compliant with tax law, designed to legally minimize taxes for the client.**

That definition clarified everything:

- quality meant accuracy and compliance
- value meant tax savings
- quantity meant how many returns I could produce

Once the product was defined, work became simple.

My job was to produce that product:

- accurately
- consistently
- in increasing volume

Income followed production.

It always does.

## How to Apply the Law of Work

Ask yourself honestly:

- What is my product?
- What defines high quality for that product?
- How is output measured?

- How many units must I produce consistently?

- What skills improve my speed and accuracy?

Then structure your days around production—not activity.

No product equals no progress.


## The Takeaway

Work is not motion.

Work is production.


Define the product.

Set the standard.


Produce consistently—at scale and with excellence.


That is how effort turns into income.

That is how income turns into wealth.

# Chapter Summary

## Law 6: The Law of Work and Production

1. Wealth is created through production—not activity or busyness.

2. Work is the disciplined production of a clearly defined product or service.

3. Real work requires three defined elements:

O a clear product

O a defined quality standard

O a measurable quantity

4. Undefined work creates confusion, conflict, and unstable income.

5. High earners define expectations before they execute.

6. Income becomes predictable when production is structured and repeatable.

7. The market pays for measurable output—not effort, motion, or intention.

8. Without a defined product, progress is impossible.

9. Consistent production at scale is what ultimately creates wealth.

**Stated simply:**

High income results from consistently producing a clearly defined product at a defined quality and in a defined quantity.

# Study & Reflection Questions

**Law 6: The Law of Work and Production**

1. Can I clearly define the exact product I am responsible for producing?

2. Is my work outcome-based—or merely activity-based?

3. What does "high quality" specifically mean for my product or service?

4. How is my output currently measured?

5. Is my income unstable because my production quantity is inconsistent or undefined?

6. Do I structure my days around production—or around staying busy?

7. What would immediately improve if I precisely defined my product, quality standard, and quantity?

# Law 7

## The Law of Habits

**Why Your Daily Actions Decide Your Financial Fate**

*"Whatsoever a man soweth, that shall he also reap."*

*— Galatians 6:7*

By now, you understand something most people never do: Wealth is not built by intention alone.

It is built by repetition.

You can know what to do. You can even want it badly.

But your habits—not your goals—determine your results. As it has often been said: Man is a creature of habit.

### What the Law of Habits Really Means

The Law of Habits states:

**Your daily habits shape your financial success or failure.**

Habits themselves are neutral.

They are neither good nor bad.

They simply produce results—consistently and reliably. Good habits compound into positive outcomes.

Bad habits compound into negative ones.

There are no exceptions.

## Aristotle Understood This Long Ago

Aristotle captured this truth simply:

*"Do the good and avoid the bad."*

That short sentence explains how habits shape a life.

You do not become wealthy by accident. You do not become poor by accident.

You take actions that lead to one outcome or the other. Repeated actions become habits.

Habits shape character.

Character influences destiny.

## Why Habits Matter More Than Motivation

Motivation is emotional. Habits are mechanical.

Motivation fades. Habits persist.

A person with poor habits will fail—even with strong motivation.

A person with good habits will succeed—even on difficult days.

Habits operate whether you are paying attention or not. That is their power.

## Wealth-Building Habits

Positive habits compound quietly over time. Examples of wealth-building habits include:

- saving a portion of income consistently
- tracking spending accurately
- investing regularly
- building valuable skills daily
- reading and learning instead of passive consumption
- creating value before expecting reward
- planning tomorrow before today ends

Each habit seems small in isolation.

Repeated daily, they reshape an entire financial life.

## Wealth-Destroying Habits

Negative habits compound just as reliably—but in the opposite direction.

Wealth-destroying habits include:

- impulse spending
- ignoring finances
- skipping budgeting
- chasing quick money
- delaying skill development
- consuming more than producing
- blaming circumstances instead of adapting

These habits rarely destroy people overnight.

They do it slowly—then all at once.

**Habits Drive Productivity**

Work requires effort.

Habits reduce resistance.

When productive actions become habitual:

- discipline becomes easier
- consistency strengthens
- progress accelerates

Habits make difficult actions easier—and easy actions automatic.

That is why disciplined people appear effortless.

They are not forcing themselves constantly.

They have trained their habits to carry the load.

## How to Apply the Law of Habits

Apply this law simply:

- identify wealth-building habits
- recognize habits that threaten wealth
- reinforce the positive
- remove or reduce the negative

As Aristotle advised:

- do the good
- avoid the bad

That alone moves you steadily toward wealth.

## The Takeaway

Habits are neutral.

They do not care what you want.

They only deliver what you repeatedly do.

If you want wealth, build habits that create it.

If you want to avoid poverty, eliminate habits that produce it.

**Small actions, repeated consistently, determine outcomes.**

# Chapter Summary

## Law 7: The Law of Habits

1. Wealth is not built by intention alone—it is built by repetition.

2. Habits are neutral; they consistently produce results without judgment.

3. Positive habits compound into wealth over time.

4. Negative habits compound into financial damage just as reliably.

5. Motivation is temporary, but habits persist regardless of emotion.

6. Repeated actions form habits, whether intentional or accidental.

7. Habits shape character, and character influences destiny.

8. Small daily behaviors determine long-term financial outcomes.

**Stated simply:**

Your financial future is the predictable result of your daily habits.

# Study & Reflection Questions

## Law 7: The Law of Habits

1. Which financial habits are currently shaping my future—for better or worse?

2. Which single small habit, if improved, would have the greatest impact on my wealth?

3. What destructive habit do I tolerate because it feels insignificant or harmless?

4. Do my daily routines support my long-term financial goals—or undermine them?

5. Am I relying on motivation, or am I building systems and habits that operate automatically?

6. Which habit should I eliminate immediately to stop negative compounding?

7. What wealth-building habit can I automate or intentionally reinforce starting today?

# Law 8

## The Law of Saving

### Why Having Surplus Drives Wealth Creation

*"Beware of little expenses; a small leak will sink a great ship."*

*— Benjamin Franklin.*

Wealth cannot be built without savings.

Every fortune—large or small—begins with a single reality:

**Income minus living expenses equals surplus.**

That surplus is savings.

Savings are the foundation of wealth.

Nearly three hundred years ago, Benjamin Franklin expressed it clearly:

"The road to wealth is paved by savings."

### The Equation That Decides Everything

Wealth is not complicated.

It begins with simple arithmetic:

**Income – Living Expenses = Surplus (Savings)**

- If the result is zero, wealth building never begins.
- If the result is negative, wealth building is destroyed.

- If the result is positive, wealth building becomes possible.

Strategies can be debated. Investment choices can be discussed.

This equation cannot.

## Why Savings Is the Most Important Variable

Savings matter more than intelligence, investment returns, timing, or opportunity.

Why?

Because wealth requires surplus. Without savings, there is:

- no capital to invest
- no margin for mistakes
- no leverage
- no path to financial independence

Savings are the seed corn.

Consume it all, and there is no harvest.

## Why Most Americans Never Build Wealth

Most Americans fail to build wealth for one reason:

They never create surplus.

This is not because they earn too little.

Over a lifetime, most Americans earn more than enough to become wealthy.

For example, investing just $100 per month starting at age 24, earning average long-term market returns, can grow into over $1 million by retirement.

People fail because:

- expenses rise with income
- spending becomes habitual
- saving is never prioritized

When income increases, lifestyle increases faster. The surplus disappears.

Without surplus, wealth is impossible.

## Surplus Enables Investment

You cannot invest money you do not have. Without savings:

- investing becomes speculation
- emergencies become crises
- opportunities pass unnoticed

With savings:

- investing becomes intentional
- risk is manageable
- opportunity is visible

Savings turn money into a tool instead of a source of stress.

## Financial Vitality: What It Means

I call this concept **financial vitality.**

Financial vitality means you can:

- absorb unexpected challenges
- act on opportunities
- make decisions calmly rather than desperately

Your level of financial vitality is determined largely by your savings rate.

High savings equals strength.

Low savings equals fragility.

Wealthy people are not just rich.

They are resilient.

## Why You Must Be Ruthless About Surplus

Surplus does not happen accidentally. It must be engineered.

That requires:

- increasing income deliberately
- controlling expenses intentionally

Politeness with costs and complacency about earnings destroy surplus.

Surplus demands discipline.

## Growing Income Without Growing Lifestyle

When income rises, most people celebrate by spending more. That is the trap.

Wealth builders do the opposite.

They:

- prioritize saving first
- delay lifestyle upgrades
- direct new income into surplus

Income growth should expand savings—not erase them.

## Reducing Expenses Without Lowering Your Life

Cutting expenses is not about deprivation.

It is about prioritization.

Every dollar spent is a vote.

You must decide:

- what supports your future
- what undermines it

Cut aggressively where spending adds little value. Spend intentionally where it truly matters.

## Savings Creates Power

Savings create power because they create options. With cash:

- you negotiate from strength
- you act quickly
- you seize undervalued opportunities

Without cash:

- you wait
- you borrow
- you miss out

Cash is not idle.

It is stored energy.

## Why Saving Comes Before Investing

This is why saving comes before investing in this book. Investing without savings is fantasy.

Saving builds:

- discipline
- patience
- opportunity

Only then does investing make sense.

## How to Apply the Law of Saving

Be honest.

Ask yourself:

- What is my current surplus?
- What percentage of my income do I save?
- Which expenses exist only because I tolerate them?
- Which income streams can I expand?

Then act.

Increase surplus deliberately.

No surplus means no wealth.

**The Takeaway**

Savings are not optional.

They are the foundation.

Income minus expenses creates surplus. Surplus creates power.

Power creates wealth.

If you want to build wealth, prioritize savings. Everything else depends on it.

# Chapter Summary

**Law 8: The Law of Saving**

1. Wealth begins with the creation of surplus.

2. Income minus living expenses equals savings.

3. Without surplus, wealth building never starts.

4. Savings is the most important variable in wealth creation.

5. Without savings, there is no investment capital, flexibility, or opportunity.

6. Financial vitality is largely determined by your savings rate.

7. Surplus must be engineered through increased income and controlled expenses.

8. Lifestyle inflation silently destroys wealth.

9. Savings create power, leverage, and options.

10. Investing without savings is fantasy.

**Stated simply:**

No surplus, no wealth. Savings are the foundation of financial power.

# Study & Reflection Questions

## Law 8: The Law of Saving

1. What is my current monthly surplus after all living expenses?

2. What percentage of my income am I consistently saving?

3. Is my lifestyle increasing faster than my income?

4. Which expenses could I eliminate or reduce without lowering my quality of life?

5. What additional income stream could most effectively increase my surplus?

6. If my income stopped tomorrow, how long could I realistically live on my savings?

7. Based on my answers, am I financially vital—or financially fragile?

# Law 9

## The Law of Investing

### How Your Money Works for You

*"Cast thy bread upon the waters: for thou shalt find it after many days."*

— *Ecclesiastes 11:1*

Saving gives you power.

But saving alone is not the goal.

Saving creates capital.

**Investing puts that capital to work.**

When done correctly, investing is where wealth begins to grow through compounding.

### What the Law of Investing Means

The Law of Investing is simple:

**Wealth is built when saved capital is invested rationally, patiently, and repeatedly.**

Investing is not about excitement, adrenaline, or fast wins.

True investing is the disciplined ownership of productive assets over time.

## Investing Is Not Gambling

One of the most damaging mistakes beginners make is confusing investing with speculation.

- day trading
- chasing price movement
- buying what is "hot"

That is not investing. That is gambling.

Benjamin Graham, the father of value investing, defined investing clearly in **The Intelligent Investor:**

"An investment operation is one which, upon thorough analysis, promises safety of principal and an adequate return. Operations not meeting these requirements are speculative."

That definition settles it.

 If safety of principal is ignored, it is not investing. If analysis is absent, it is not investing.

If success depends on guessing short-term prices, it is not investing.

## Why Most People Lose Money

Most people fail at investing for the same reasons. They:

- speculate instead of analyze
- trade instead of own
- react emotionally instead of thinking rationally

Speculation appeals to emotion.

Investing appeals to reason.

The market eventually punishes emotion and rewards discipline.

## The Investor's Mindset

The purpose of investing is **not** to get rich quickly. The purpose is to build wealth **predictably.**

This mindset:

- protects capital
- reduces urgency
- encourages patience

Desperation is the enemy of good investing.

## Warren Buffett's Circle of Competence

One of the most important investing principles ever articulated is Warren Buffett's Circle of Competence.

You do not need to understand everything.

You need to understand **a few things extremely well.** Your circle includes businesses where:

- you understand how money is made
- you can identify what drives success or failure
- you can explain why the business will remain relevant

Outside that circle, you are guessing.

And guessing is not investing.

## Why the Size of the Circle Doesn't Matter

Many people think success requires:

- broad knowledge
- constant exposure to new ideas

It does not.

Buffett emphasized this repeatedly:

What matters is not the size of your circle— but knowing its boundaries.

A small circle, deeply understood, is far more powerful than a large one filled with uncertainty.

## Why Staying Inside the Circle Creates Patience

Understanding what you own creates conviction.

Conviction filters out noise.

Noise creates panic.

Panic destroys compounding.

Patience is not emotional strength.

It is the by-product of understanding.

## How I Applied This Law: NVIDIA

In late 2022, ChatGPT revealed a clear technological breakthrough. I asked one question:

**What makes this possible?**

The answer kept pointing to NVIDIA.

Its chips powered large-scale AI training.

At the same time, the stock was recovering from poor performance.

This was not a trade.

It was a long-term investment thesis.

I invested heavily around $200 per share (pre-split). I did not trade in and out.

I did not hedge. I did not panic.

Why?

Because I understood:

- the technology
- the demand
- the economics
- the long-term trajectory

That investment has since grown over 1,200%.

Not because of luck.

But because I saved first, studied deeply, invested rationally, and waited.

## Investors vs. Gamblers

Gamblers focus on:

- price movement
- excitement
- constant action

Investors focus on:

- value
- durability
- cash flow
- long-term ownership

Gamblers rely on luck.

Investors rely on process.

## How to Apply the Law of Investing

Before you invest, ask:

- Do I understand how this asset produces value?
- Will it still matter in 5–10 years?
- What risks could destroy it?
- Am I informed—or just excited?

If you cannot answer clearly, step back.

Staying inside your circle is not limiting. It is liberating.

## The Takeaway

Saving creates capital.

Investing compounds it.

When you invest rationally, patiently, and within your circle of competence, wealth stops being a matter of luck.

It becomes the result of process. That is the Law of Investing.

# Chapter Summary

## Law 9: The Law of Investing

1. Saving creates capital; investing is what multiplies it.

2. True investing is the rational, long-term ownership of productive assets.

3. Proper investing requires three elements:

   - thorough analysis
   - safety of principal
   - an adequate return

4. Speculation relies on price movement; investing relies on underlying value.

5. Staying within your circle of competence protects capital and reduces risk.

6. Understanding what you own creates conviction.

7. Conviction enables patience during market volatility.

8. Patience allows compounding to work.

9. Cash provides the freedom to invest rationally instead of emotionally.

10. Long-term wealth is built through process—not excitement.

## Stated simply:

Wealth grows when saved capital is invested rationally, within your circle of competence, and held patiently over time.

# Study & Reflection Questions

**Law 9: The Law of Investing**

1. Am I truly investing—or am I speculating?

2. Do I fully understand the assets I currently own?

3. Are my investment decisions based on analysis—or on excitement and headlines?

4. What clearly falls inside my circle of competence?

5. Which investments am I holding outside that circle, and why?

6. Do I have sufficient savings to invest patiently rather than urgently?

7. Would I be comfortable owning my investments for the next five to ten years?

# Law 10

## The Law of Patience

### Why Time Is the Ultimate Wealth Advantage

*"And let us not grow weary in doing good, for in due season we shall reap the harvest."*

— *Galatian 6:9*

By now, you understand how wealth is built. You know how to:

- create value
- produce consistently
- establish effective habits
- save diligently
- invest rationally

And yet, this is where many people still fail. Not because they are wrong—

but because they are impatient.

## What the Law of Patience Means

The Law of Patience states:

**Wealth is created by allowing sound decisions to compound over time.**

Patience is not passive.

It is not waiting and hoping.

Patience is **active discipline**—the discipline to stay the course while results are still invisible.

## Building Wealth Takes Time

Rome was not built in a day. Neither is wealth.

Rome required planning, discipline, and sustained effort over time. Wealth is built the same way.

It grows:

- year by year
- decision by decision
- habit by habit

Those who demand immediate results abandon the foundations of lasting success.

## Why Impatience Destroys Wealth

Most people do not lose money because they are wrong. They lose money because they are impatient.

They:

- exit too early
- overtrade
- chase quick results
- confuse volatility with risk

Impatience interrupts compounding.

Markets consistently punish it.

## Why Impatience Leads to Get-Rich-Quick Schemes

A lack of patience prevents wealth.

When people stop trusting time, they demand results now. That mindset drives them toward:

- day trading
- futures and leveraged products
- currency speculation
- speculative cycles like crypto manias

These strategies feel exciting.

They feel active.

 But they do not work.

They are **get-poor-eventually schemes.**

## A True Story: The Cost of Impatience

This lesson is personal.

Over the past few years, I gave my son nearly $100,000 to invest alongside me during the AI boom.

The opportunity was clear.

Artificial intelligence was a platform shift—not a fad.

I invested patiently and rationally.

He chose speed.

He traded aggressively using futures.

Today, that money is gone.

More damaging than the loss is the emotional cost.

He is discouraged and deeply shaken.

## What Impatience Really Cost

Here is the hardest truth:

Had he invested patiently and held the same assets I did, he would be a millionaire today. No special skill required.

No perfect timing. Just patience.

Impatience did not only cost money.

It destroyed years of compounding that can never be recovered.

## Compounding Is Quiet—At First

Compounding does not announce itself. Early on:

- progress feels slow
- gains appear modest
- effort goes unnoticed

That is normal.

Rome did not look like Rome while it was being built. Neither does wealth.

Impatience prevents people from ever reaching the stage where progress accelerates.

## Why Patience Is a Competitive Advantage

Most people want results now.

They chase:

- immediate profits

- fast validation
- constant action

That impatience creates opportunity—for those willing to wait.

Patience allows you to:

- hold valuable assets
- ignore short-term noise
- make rational decisions
- let time work in your favor

In a world addicted to speed, patience is rare—and powerful.

## What Patience Did for Me

I did not become wealthy overnight.

I stayed consistent.

I:

- saved year after year
- invested thoughtfully
- reinvested returns
- avoided unnecessary changes

While others jumped in and out, I stayed committed. Patience paid off.

## Patience Is Not Passive

This is critical.

Patience does **not** mean doing nothing.

It means acting correctly—and then allowing time to work. If fundamentals change, you adjust.

If they remain sound, you stay invested.

Impatience reacts constantly.

Patience acts deliberately.

## How to Apply the Law of Patience

To grow wealth:

- focus on long-term outcomes, not quick wins
- judge decisions by logic, not short-term results
- avoid constant changes
- give good decisions time to compound If the foundation is sound, time will do the rest.

## The Takeaway

Rome was not built in a day.

Wealth is not either.

When sound decisions are combined with discipline and patience, results follow.

Those who wait intelligently outperform those who rush.

That is the Law of Patience.

# Chapter Summary

**Law 10: The Law of Patience**

1. Wealth is created by allowing sound decisions to compound over time.

2. Patience is active discipline—not passive waiting.

3. Rome was not built in a day, and neither is wealth.

4. Impatience destroys compounding through overtrading and premature exits.

5. Get-rich-quick strategies feel exciting but usually end in loss.

6. The true cost of impatience is the permanent loss of years of compounding.

7. Compounding appears slow at first, then becomes powerful over time.

8. Patience becomes a competitive advantage in a world addicted to speed.

9. Patience acts deliberately, while impatience reacts repeatedly.

10. Long-term consistency is what ultimately produces financial independence.

**Stated simply:**

Correct decisions, combined with time, create wealth. Impatience interrupts the process.

# Study & Reflection Questions

## Law 10: The Law of Patience

1. Where in my financial life am I trying to rush results that require time?

2. Have I sold too early or changed strategies too often—and what prompted those decisions?

3. Which "get-rich-quick" ideas have tempted me the most, and why?

4. Do I confuse short-term volatility with long-term danger?

5. Do I truly have a long-term plan—or am I acting on short-term urges?

6. What would likely happen if I simply made sound investments for the next five to ten years?

7. What one action can I take today to strengthen patience and long-term discipline?

<br>

# Law 11

## The Law of Environment

### Why Your Surroundings Decide Your Success

*"Associate yourself with people of good quality, for it is better to be alone than in bad company."*

— *Booker T. Washington*

By now, you understand that wealth is built from the inside out:

Desire.

Reality.

Responsibility.

Value.

Skills.

Work.

Habits.

Saving.

Investing.

Patience.

Yet even with sound decisions and discipline in place, one force can either accelerate your progress—or quietly undo it.

That force is your environment.

Have you noticed how the people, information, and settings around you shape your habits—often without your awareness?

## What the Law of Environment Means

The Law of Environment states:

**Your environment shapes your behavior—and your behavior determines your results.**

Psychologists have long observed that much of human behavior is automatic rather than consciously chosen.

Whether the percentage is exact or not, the truth remains:

Most daily actions are responses to environment, not deliberate decisions.

## Why You Must Guard What Shapes You

One of the most practical pieces of wisdom ever recorded states:

"Guard your heart with all diligence,

for out of it flow the issues of life."

—Proverbs 4:23

This is not only spiritual guidance, it is economic instruction. Your environment influences:

- how you think
- what you tolerate
- the standards you accept

- the goals you pursue
- the person you become

If you want to build wealth, you must guard what shapes your thinking.

## What the Law of Environment Really Means

The law is simple:

Your outcomes are shaped by what you repeatedly expose yourself to.

Not once.

Repeatedly.

Your surroundings quietly influence your:

- expectations
- patience
- discipline
- standards

Most people passively accept their environment—and deal with the consequences later.

## What Makes Up Your Environment

Your environment includes:

- the people you spend time with
- the conversations you hear
- the media you consume
- the behaviors you tolerate Human beings adapt.

Over time, we unconsciously conform to:

- social norms
- repeated opinions
- accepted behaviors

If your environment normalizes:

- overspending
- excuses
- short-term thinking

Those behaviors become automatic.

If it reinforces:

- discipline
- learning
- delayed gratification Those behaviors become natural.

Environment works—even when you are not paying attention.

## Guarding Your Heart Is a Wealth Strategy

"Guarding your heart" means protecting what you allow into your mind.

This includes:

- conversations
- media
- opinions
- social circles

What you repeatedly consume becomes your internal dialogue.

Your internal dialogue drives decisions.

Poor inputs produce poor decisions.

Poor decisions destroy wealth.

**Who You Associate with Matters More Than You Think**

My father used to say:

*"Show me your friends, and I will show you your future."*

People influence you—even when they say nothing. Attitudes around you affect:

- how you view opportunity
- how you assess risk
- what you consider normal

If those around, you:

- dismiss saving
- chase short-term gains
- speculate constantly
- complain habitually

You will feel pressure to conform—or slowly drift.

Wealth builders are often lonely early on because they refuse to drift.

## The Hidden Cost of the Wrong Environment

A poor environment:

- weakens patience
- undermines discipline
- encourages destructive behavior It makes:
- speculation seems intelligent
- consumption feels safe
- impatience sounds reasonable

Many people do not fail financially because of bad decisions. They absorb bad thinking.

## Why Cutting Is Sometimes Necessary

This is where the cutting rule applies again.

To protect your future, you must cut:

- relationships that hold you back
- information that feeds fear or greed
- environments that encourage impatience

This is not cruelty.

It is self-preservation.

## Design an Environment That Protects Patience

Wealth requires long-term thinking.

Your environment must support it.

- reduce exposure to hype
- ignore market noise
- seek disciplined thinkers

- value wisdom over excitement

Patience is fragile.

Environment either protects it—or destroys it.

## A Bad Environment Cannot Be Outsmarted

Many believe they are strong enough to resist influence. They are not.

No one is.

Environment beats willpower.

That is why guarding your environment is not optional.

It is essential.

## How to Apply the Law of Environment

Ask yourself honestly:

- Who has the greatest influence on my thinking?
- What ideas am I exposed to most often?
- Which conversations leave me misinformed or agitated?
- What inputs encourage impatience or speculation?

Then act deliberately. Choose environments that:

- reinforce discipline
- normalize patience
- reward long-term thinking

## The Takeaway

Wealth does not require only good decisions.

It requires protection from bad influence.

Guard your inputs.

Guard your associations.

Guard your environment.

Because of this, the decisions that shape your life—and your wealth.

That is the Law of Environment.

# Chapter Summary

## Law 11: The Law of Environment

1. Your environment shapes your behavior.

2. Behavior determines results.

3. Most daily actions are automatic responses to surroundings rather than conscious choices.

4. Repeated exposure establishes expectations, standards, and norms.

5. "Guard your heart" is both spiritual wisdom and practical economic advice.

6. Poor environments normalize overspending, impatience, and speculation.

7. Disciplined environments normalize saving, learning, and long-term thinking.

8. No amount of willpower can overcome a consistently bad environment.

9. Cutting harmful influences is an act of self-preservation, not cruelty.

10. Building wealth requires actively protecting mental, social, and informational inputs.

## Stated simply:

Your environment shapes your behavior. Guard it—or it will shape you.

# Study & Reflection Questions

**Law 11: The Law of Environment**

1. Who most strongly influences my financial thinking and attitudes?

2. What conversations do I repeatedly expose myself to?

3. Does my environment encourage saving and discipline—or spending and indulgence?

4. Does it reward patience and long-term thinking—or hype and urgency?

5. What media inputs most strongly shape my financial decisions?

6. Is there a relationship, habit, or influence that may need distance or boundaries?

7. What single change to my environment would most strengthen my discipline?

# Law 12

## The Law of Wisdom

### Why Building Wealth Requires Sound Judgment

*"Wisdom is the principal thing, Therefore, get wisdom, and with thy getting get understanding,*

*— Proverbs 4:7*

Every law before this one can be learned. Desire can be cultivated.

Skills can be developed.

Habits can be installed.

Money can be saved and invested.

But wisdom is different.

Wisdom governs the proper use of all resources.

Without it, wealth cannot be built—or kept.

### What the Law of Wisdom Means

The Law of Wisdom is best understood through Aristotle.

In **Nicomachean Ethics**, Aristotle defined practical wisdom as the ability to:

- know what should be done
- at the right time
- in the right way

- under the right circumstances
- for the purpose of living well

Wisdom is not intelligence.

It is not education.

It is not information.

**Wisdom is judgment applied to action.**

And here is the truth most people avoid:

Poor decisions do not create wealth.

Foolish decisions create predictable failure.

 Stupid choices lead to stupid actions.

Stupid actions lead to predictable outcomes.

Reality does not forgive foolishness—especially with money.

## Why This Law Governs All the Others

You can:

- work hard
- save consistently
- invest actively

And still fail—if your judgment is poor.

Wisdom governs:

- which goals you pursue
- which opportunities you avoid
- when you act
- when you wait

Without wisdom:

- desire becomes reckless
- skills are misapplied
- investing turns into gambling
- opportunity turns into loss

You may make money.

But you will lose it through bad decisions.

## Ancient Wisdom, Modern Truth

Aristotle understood this long before modern finance.

He taught that wisdom is the highest practical virtue because it directs all action.

Not intention.

Not theory.

Action.

Wise people choose well.

Unwise people repeat mistakes—and blame luck.

## Unwise Decisions Are Expensive

Examples of poor judgment include:

- investing blindly
- ignoring risk
- chasing fast profits
- refusing to learn
- repeating the same mistakes

These are not accidents.

They are failures of judgment.

Effort does not determine long-term results. Judgment does.

## Wisdom Is Often About Restraint

One of the clearest signs of wisdom is knowing what not to do. Wisdom says:

- "This opportunity looks attractive, but it is not sound."
- "I do not understand this well enough to participate."
- "This is not the right time."

The ability to act does not mean you should act.

Restraint protects wealth more reliably than boldness.

## How Wisdom Is Built

Wisdom is developed through:

- real-world experience
- honest evaluation of outcomes
- correcting mistakes
- learning from those more experienced

Wise people adjust.

Unwise people repeat.

That difference compounds over a lifetime.

As Machiavelli observed:

*"The wise man does at once what the fool does finally."*

## How to Apply the Law of Wisdom

Before major financial decisions, ask:

- Is this decision rational—or emotional?
- Do I understand the consequences?
- What if I am wrong?
- Am I repeating a past mistake?

Wealth is not built by cleverness.

It is built by avoiding stupidity consistently.

## The Final Takeaway

You do not need to be a genius to become wealthy.

But you cannot become wealthy by being careless, impulsive, or foolish.

You cannot build wealth by making bad decisions.

You cannot keep wealth repeating them.

Wisdom is the habit of making good decisions—consistently and deliberately. It is the governing law.

# Chapter Summary

**Law 12: The Law of Wisdom**

1. Wisdom governs the proper use of all wealth-building tools.

2. Wisdom is judgment applied to action—not intelligence or education.

3. Poor decisions lead to predictable financial failure.

4. Without wisdom, desire becomes reckless and investing becomes gambling.

5. Judgment determines whether money is built—or lost.

6. Wise people learn and adjust; unwise people repeat mistakes.

7. Restraint is often more powerful than boldness.

8. Wealth is built by consistently avoiding foolish decisions.

9. Wisdom compounds over a lifetime through experience and reflection.

10. Wisdom is the ultimate law because it governs all the others.

**Stated simply:**

You cannot build or keep wealth without sound judgment.

# Study & Reflection Questions

## Law 12: The Law of Wisdom

1. What recent financial decision reflects sound wisdom—or a lack of it?

2. Do I consistently pause thinking before making major financial moves?

3. Am I repeating patterns that have previously cost me money or opportunity?

4. What decision am I currently rationalizing instead of evaluating honestly?

5. Do I actively seek counsel from people with more experience and proven judgment?

6. Where in my life would restraint be wiser than immediate action?

7. If wisdom means choosing well consistently, where must I improve right now?

# Closing

## The Complete Blueprint

**You now have the full framework:**

1. Burning Desire

2. Reality

3. Responsibility

4. Value

5. Skills

6. Work

7. Habits

8. Saving

9. Investing

10. Patience

11. Environment

12. Wisdom

These twelve laws are not theories.

They are not motivation.

They are principles.

Live by them—not perfectly, but deliberately—and wealth stops being mysterious.

It becomes the natural outcome of sound judgment, practiced consistently, over time.

That is the blueprint.

# Conclusion

## Rational Living Creates Wealth

You have now seen the complete blueprint.

Not theories.

Not opinions.

**Laws.**

They are simple—but not easy.

Clear—but not always comfortable.

And that is precisely why they work.

**The Twelve Laws in One Truth**

Wealth is not built by chance.

It is built by individuals who:

- desire something deeply
- face reality honestly
- take full responsibility
- create value deliberately
- master useful skills
- produce consistently
- build empowering habits
- save with intention
- invest rationally
- wait patiently
- design their environment
- and exercise wisdom

Ignore even one law, and progress slows. Ignore several, and wealth collapses.

Live by them consistently—and wealth becomes the natural result.

## Why Most People Never Become Wealthy

It is not because they cannot. It is because they fail to:

- think rationally
- delay gratification
- remove harmful influences
- avoid poor decisions

You cannot become wealthy by making unwise choices.

And you cannot remain wealthy by repeating them.

Wealth demands judgment.

That is why wisdom is the final law.

## The Good News

You do not need to be extraordinary to build wealth.

You do not need rare talent, perfect timing, or complete knowledge.

What you do need is:

- **discipline over impulse** — choosing control over comfort
- **patience over urgency** — allowing time to work

- **reason over emotion** — thinking clearly under pressure

Above all, you need the courage to act consistently.

Progress comes not from perfection, but from steady, deliberate effort over time.

## A Final Thought

Rome was not built in a day.

Neither is wealth.

But Rome was built deliberately—stone by stone.

So is financial independence.

Live by these laws—not perfectly, but persistently—and your life will change.

Not overnight.

But permanently.

## Your Next Step

Close this book and do one thing:

Create a plan to apply these laws to your financial life—starting today.

Then act.

Wealth is not a mystery.

Over time, it is the natural result of living rationally.

# A Call to Rational Living

Rational living begins with clear thinking, intentional action, and decisions grounded in objective reality—not emotion, impulse, or illusion.

That is the foundation of everything you have just read.

You now understand the **Twelve Laws of Wealth Building.** You know the principles.

You see the structure.

You recognize the pattern.

The question is no longer what to do.

The question is whether you will live it.

Wealth is not built by wishing.

It is not built by blaming.

It is not built by drifting.

It is built by thinking.

## What It Means to Live Rationally

To live rationally is to:

- see reality as it is—not as you want it to be
- take full responsibility for outcomes—without excuse
- create value deliberately
- master useful skills
- produce consistently
- install disciplined habits

- generate surplus
- invest with judgment
- allow time to compound wise decisions
- guard your environment
- exercise wisdom in every major choice

Rational living is not dramatic.

It is steady. It is quiet.

It is disciplined.

## The Rational Wealth Builder

Most people drift through life—reacting to circumstances, chasing trends, absorbing the thinking of others.

A rational wealth builder does the opposite.

He chooses direction.

He measures results.

He adjusts when wrong.

He compounds what works.

He eliminates what doesn't.

He does not depend on hype. He does not depend on luck. He does not depend on rescue.

He depends on principles.

**The Result of Rational Living**

Rational living creates financial strength.

Financial strength creates independence.

Independence creates peace.

A calm river.

That is what this book ultimately offers. Not just money—

but control.

And control comes from alignment with reality.

**The Choice**

From this moment forward, there are only two paths:

Live by these laws.

Or drift without them.

One path compounds.

The other consumes.

Choose deliberately. Think clearly.

Act consistently. Build patiently.

And let time reward discipline—

the way it always does.

# The Wealth Builder's Oath

*Before continuing, read this oath aloud. Commitment is strengthened when words are spoken.*

I accept reality as it is.

I take full responsibility for my financial life.

I will not blame markets, governments, employers, or circumstances.

I will build value before I demand reward.

I will master skills the market respects.

I will define my work and produce consistently.

I will save before I spend.

I will create surplus—and protect it.

I will invest rationally, within my circle of competence.

I will reject speculation and emotional decision-making.

I will allow time to compound my disciplined choices.

I will guard my environment and protect my thinking.

I will choose wisdom over impulse.

I understand that wealth is not luck.

It is the result of alignment with immutable laws.

I commit to living by these laws—

not occasionally,

but consistently.

My financial future will not be accidental.

It will be constructed.

Deliberately. Rationally.

Patiently.

And I accept the responsibility that comes with that choice.

**— Robert Malone**

# About the Author

Robert Malone is a CPA, investor, entrepreneur, and wealth-building strategist who has spent more than three decades studying and applying the principles that govern financial success.

He was not born into wealth. He was born into discipline.

Raised in a working-class family, Robert grew up watching his father pick cotton for two dollars a day. One day in the fields, his father said something that would shape the rest of his life:

*"Son, it's your job to get this family out of poverty."*

Robert did not fully understand the weight of those words at the time. But he never forgot them.

From that moment forward, wealth was no longer a wish—it became a responsibility.

By age 31, through aggressive saving, disciplined skill development, business ownership, real estate investing, and rational capital allocation, Robert became a millionaire. Since then, he has built businesses, acquired income-producing assets, invested in equities, and advised clients on tax strategy and long-term financial planning.

What distinguishes Robert's approach is not tactics.

It is structure.

Drawing from Aristotle, Marcus Aurelius, Benjamin Graham, Warren Buffett, and decades of lived experience, Robert teaches that wealth is not luck. It is the predictable result of living in alignment with immutable principles.

He believes:

- Income follows value.
- Value follows skill.
- Skills follow discipline.
- Discipline follows choice.

*The 12 Laws of Wealth Building* represents the distilled framework of lessons learned through rational decision-making, production, saving, investing, patience, and practical wisdom.

This book is not theory. It is tested structure.

Robert believes financial independence is not reserved for the gifted or fortunate. It is available to anyone willing to think clearly, act deliberately, and live consistently by sound principles.

His mission is simple:

To help others build wealth rationally, deliberately, and permanently.

This book is the foundation.

The work is yours.